MW00683297

Paths to College and Career
Case Study

How Working Conditions Change:
Chávez and the UFW

A Wiley Brand

EXPEDITIONARY
LEARNING

GRADE 7, MODULE 2A: UNIT 2, LESSON 1

Entry Task
Working Conditions: Then and Now

Name:		Date:	

Directions: Study the two images of working conditions and answer the questions below.

1. Clearly, working conditions in textile mills have changed since the 1800s. What specific changes do you see in these photos? What remains similar?

    _____

    _____

    _____

    _____

2. Why have working conditions changed?

    _____

    _____

    _____

    _____

3. Who is responsible for changing working conditions?

    _____

    _____

    _____

    _____

Common Core ELA Curriculum

GRADE 7, MODULE 2A: UNIT 2, LESSON 1

....

Agents of Change Anchor Chart

Workers	Governments

Consumers	Businesses

EXPEDITIONARY
LEARNING

GRADE 7, MODULE 2A: UNIT 2, LESSON 1

Building Background Knowledge Worksheet

Name:		Date:	

Use this worksheet to note what you learned about César Chávez's life and work.

A. EARLY LIFE	
Childhood	
Young adult	

B. ORGANIZING UNITED FARM WORKERS	
Why he formed it	
What success the UFW had	

C. LASTING LEGACY

Common Core ELA Curriculum

Directions: César Chávez says, "Our opponents must understand that it's not just the union we have built. Unions, like other institutions, can come and go—but we're more than institutions."

Read the following quotes and discuss how Chávez illustrates that a union is "more than an institution." What does he say it is?

"And one thing I hear most often from Hispanics, regardless of age or position, and from many non-Hispanics as well, is that the [United Farm Workers union] gave them the hope that they could succeed and the inspiration to work for change."

"Our union will forever exist as an empowering force among Chicanos in the Southwest. That means our power and our influence will grow and not diminish."

"Regardless of what the future holds for the union, regardless of what the future holds for farmworkers, our accomplishments cannot be undone. La causa, our cause, doesn't have to be experienced twice."

EXPEDITIONARY
LEARNING

GRADE 7, MODULE 2A: UNIT 2, LESSON 2

Commonwealth Club Address

ODELL
EDUCATION

Updated June 2013

Commonwealth Club Address

San Francisco, November 9, 1984

Cesar Chavez

Thank you very much, Mr. Lee, Mrs. Black, ladies and gentlemen.   P1

Twenty-one years ago, this last September, on a lonely stretch of railroad track   P2
paralleling U.S. Highway 101 near Salinas, 32 Bracero farm workers lost their lives in a
tragic accident. The Braceros had been imported from Mexico to work on California farms.

5   They died when their bus, which was converted from a flatbed truck, drove in front of a
freight train. Conversion of the bus had not been approved by any government agency.
The driver had **tunnel vision**. Most of the bodies laid unidentified for days. No one,
including the grower who employed the workers, even knew their names. Today,
thousands of farm workers live under **savage** conditions, beneath trees and amid

10 garbage and human excrement near tomato fields in San Diego County; tomato fields,
which use the most modern farm technology. Vicious rats gnaw at them as they sleep.
They walk miles to buy food at inflated prices and they carry in water from irrigation
ditches.

Child labor is still common in many farm areas. As much as 30 percent of Northern   P3
15 California's garlic harvesters are underage children. Kids as young as six years old
have voted in states, conducted union elections, since they qualified as workers. Some
800,000 underage children work with their families harvesting crops across America.
Babies born to **migrant** workers suffer 25 percent higher infant **mortality** rates than the

---

tunnel vision: defective sight in which objects not in
the center field of vision cannot be properly seen
savage: harsh

migrant: moving from place to
place in search of work
mortality: death

page 1

EXPEDITIONARY LEARNING

GRADE 7, MODULE 2A: UNIT 2, LESSON 2
....
Commonwealth Club Address

Updated June 2013

20 rest of the population. Malnutrition among migrant workers' children is 10 times higher than the national rate. Farm workers' average life expectancy is still 49 years, compared to 73 years for the average American.

All my life, I have been driven by one dream, one goal, one vision: to overthrow a **P4** farm labor system in this nation that treats farm workers as if they were not important human beings. Farm workers are not agricultural **implements**; they are not beasts of 25 burden to be used and discarded. That dream was born in my youth, it was nurtured in my early days of organizing. It has flourished. It has been attacked.

I'm not very different from anyone else who has ever tried to accomplish something **P5** with his life. My motivation comes from my personal life, from watching what my mother and father went through when I was growing up, from what we experienced as 30 migrant workers in California. That dream, that vision grew from my own experience with racism, with hope, with a desire to be treated fairly, and to see my people treated as human beings and not as **chattel**. It grew from anger and rage, emotions I felt 40 years ago when people of my color were denied the right to see a movie or eat at a restaurant in many parts of California. It grew from the frustration and humiliation I felt as a boy who 35 couldn't understand how the growers could abuse and exploit farm workers when there were so many of us and so few of them.

Later in the 50s, I experienced a different kind of exploitation. In San Jose, in Los **P6** Angeles and in other urban communities, we, the Mexican-American people, were dominated by a majority that was **Anglo**. I began to realize what other minority people 40 had discovered; that the only answer, the only hope was in organizing. More of us had to become citizens, we had to register to vote, and people like me had to develop the skills it would take to organize, to educate, to help empower the **Chicano** people.

---

implements: tools
chattel: property or personal possession

Anglo: a white American not of Hispanic descent
Chicano: an American of Mexican descent

page 2

Used with permission from Odell Education

GRADE 7, MODULE 2A: UNIT 2, LESSON 2

Commonwealth Club Address

I spent many years before we founded the **union** learning how to work with people.   **P7**
We experienced some successes in voter registration, in politics, in battling racial
45   discrimination -- successes in an era where Black Americans were just beginning to **assert**
their civil rights and when political awareness among Hispanics was almost non-existent.
But deep in my heart, I knew I could never be happy unless I tried organizing the farm
workers. I didn't know if I would succeed, but I had to try.

All Hispanics, urban and rural, young and old, are connected to the farm workers'   **P8**
50   experience. We had all lived through the fields, or our parents had. We shared that
common humiliation. How could we progress as a people even if we lived in the cities,
while the farm workers, men and women of our color, were condemned to a life without
pride? How could we progress as a people while the farm workers, who symbolized our
history in this land, were denied self-respect? How could our people believe that their
55   children could become lawyers and doctors and judges and business people while this
shame, this injustice, was permitted to continue?

Those who attack our union often say it's not really a union. It's something else, a   **P9**
social movement, a civil rights movement -- it's something dangerous. They're half
right. The United Farm Workers is first and foremost a union, a union like any other, a
60   union that either produces for its members on the bread-and-butter issues or doesn't
survive. But the UFW has always been something more than a union, although it's never
been dangerous, if you believe in the Bill of Rights. The UFW was the beginning. We
attacked that historical source of shame and infamy that our people in this country lived
with. We attacked that injustice, not by complaining, not by seeking handouts, not by
65   becoming soldiers in the war on poverty; we organized!

---

union: an organization of workers formed to   **assert**: claim
advance the interests of its members

page 3

Used with permission from Odell Education

Farm workers acknowledge we had allowed ourselves to become victims in a   **P10**
democratic society, a society where majority rules and collective bargaining are
supposed to be more than academic theories and political rhetoric. And by addressing
this historical problem, we created confidence and pride and hope in an entire people's
70 ability to create the future. The UFW survival, its existence, were not in doubt in my mind
when the time began to come.

After the union became visible, when Chicanos started entering college in greater   **P11**
numbers, when Hispanics began running for public office in greater numbers, when
our people started asserting their rights on a broad range of issues and in many
75 communities across this land. The union survival, its very existence, sent out a signal to all
Hispanics that we were fighting for our dignity, that we were challenging and overcoming
injustice, that we were empowering the least educated among us, the poorest among us.
The message was clear. If it could happen in the fields, it could happen anywhere: in the
cities, in the courts, in the city councils, in the state legislatures. I didn't really appreciate it
80 at the time, but the coming of our union signaled the start of great changes among
Hispanics that are only now beginning to be seen.

I've traveled through every part of this nation. I have met and spoken with thousands **P12**
of Hispanics from every walk of life, from every social and economic class. And one
thing I hear most often from Hispanics, regardless of age or position, and from many non-
85 Hispanics as well, is that the farm workers gave them the hope that they could succeed
and the inspiration to work for change.

From time to time, you will hear our opponents declare that the union is weak, that   **P13**
the union has no support, that the union has not grown fast enough. Our obituary
has been written many times. How ironic it is that the same forces that argue so
90 passionately that the union is not influential are the same forces that continue to fight us
so hard.

page 4

The union's power in agriculture has nothing to do with the number of farm workers **P14** on the union contract. It has nothing to do with the farm workers' ability to contribute to democratic politicians. It doesn't even have much to do with our ability to

95 conduct successful boycotts. The very fact of our existence forces an entire industry, unionized and non-unionized, to spend millions of dollars year after year on increased wages, on improved working conditions, and on benefits for workers. If we were so weak and unsuccessful, why do the growers continue to fight us with such passion? Because as long as we continue to exist, farm workers will benefit from our existence, even if they

100 don't work under union contract. It doesn't really matter whether we have 100,000 or 500,000 members. In truth, hundreds of thousands of farm workers in California and in other states are better off today because of our work. And Hispanics across California and the nation who don't work in agriculture are better off today because of what the farm workers taught people about organization, about pride and strength, about seizing

105 control over their own lives.

Tens of thousands of children and grandchildren of farm workers and the children **P15** and grandchildren of poor Hispanics are moving out of the fields and out of the barrios and into the professions and into business and into politics, and that movement cannot be reversed. Our union will forever exist as an empowering force among Chicanos

110 in the Southwest. That means our power and our influence will grow and not diminish.

Two major trends give us hope and encouragement. First, our union has returned to **P16** a tried and tested weapon in the farm workers non-violent arsenal: the **boycott**. After the **Agricultural Labor Relations Act** became law in California in 1975, we **dismantled** our boycott to work with the law. During the early and mid '70s millions of Americans

115 supported our boycotts. After 1975, we redirected our efforts from the boycott to

boycott: refusal by a group to buy goods or services to show support for a cause **dismantle**: take apart	**Agricultural Labor Relations Act**: law enacted by the state of California in 1975 to protect, among other things, the right of farm workers to self-organize and negotiate the conditions of their employment

page 5

Used with permission from Odell Education

Common Core ELA Curriculum

organizing and winning elections under the law. That law helped farm workers make progress in overcoming poverty and injustice.

At companies where farm workers are protected by union contracts, we have made **P17** progress in overcoming child labor, in overcoming miserable wages and working 120 conditions, in overcoming sexual harassment of women workers, in overcoming discrimination in employment, in overcoming dangerous pesticides, which poison our people and poison the food we all eat. Where we have organized these injustices soon passed in history, but under Republican Governor George Deukmejian, the law that guarantees our right to organize no longer protects farm workers; it doesn't work 125 anymore.

In 1982, corporate growers gave Deukmejian one million dollars to run for governor **P18** of California. Since he took office, Deukmejian has paid back his debt to the growers with the blood and sweat of California farm workers. Instead of enforcing the law as it was written against those who break it, Deukmejian invites growers who break the law to seek 130 relief from governor's appointees. What does all this mean for farm workers? It means that the right to vote in free elections is a sham. It means the right to talk freely about the union among your fellow workers on the job is a cruel hoax. It means that the right to be free from threats and intimidation by growers is an empty promise. It means that the right to sit down and negotiate with your employer as equals across the bargaining table and 135 not as peons in the fields is a fraud. It means that thousands of farm workers, who are owed millions of dollars in back pay because their employers broke the law, are still waiting for their checks. It means that 36,000 farm workers, who voted to be represented by the United Farm Workers in free elections, are still waiting for contracts from growers who refuse to bargain in good faith. It means that for farm workers child labor will 140 continue. It means that infant mortality will continue. It means that malnutrition among children will continue. It means the short life expectancy and the inhuman living and working conditions will continue.

page 6

GRADE 7, MODULE 2A: UNIT 2, LESSON 2
....
Commonwealth Club Address

Updated June 2013

Are these make-believe threats? Are they exaggerations? Ask the farm workers who **P19** are waiting for the money they lost because the growers broke the law. Ask the farm

145 workers who are still waiting for growers to bargain in good faith and sign contracts. Ask the farm workers who have been fired from their jobs because they spoke out for the union. Ask the farm workers who have been threatened with physical violence because they support the UFW, and ask the family of Rene Lopez, the young farm worker from Fresno who was shot to death last year because he supported the union as he came out of

150 a voting booth. Ask the farm workers who watch their children go hungry in this land of wealth and promise. Ask the farm workers who see their lives eaten away by poverty and suffering.

These tragic events force farm workers to declare a new international boycott of **P20** California grapes, except the three percent of grapes produced under union contract.

155 That is why we are asking Americans, once again, to join the farm workers by boycotting California grapes. The newest Harris Poll revealed that 17 million Americans boycotted grapes. We are convinced that those people and that goodwill have not disappeared. That segment of the population which makes the boycotts work are the Hispanics, the Blacks, the other minorities, our friends in labor and the Church. But it is also an entire generation

160 of young Americans who matured politically and socially in the '60s and the '70s, millions of people for whom boycotting grapes and other products became a socially accepted pattern of behavior. If you were young, Anglo and/or near campers during the late '60s and early '70s, chances are you supported farm workers.

15 years later, the men and women of that generation are alive and well. They are in **P21**

165 their mid 30s and 40s. They are pursuing professional careers, their **disposable** incomes are relatively high, but they are still inclined to respond to an appeal from farm workers. The union's mission still has meaning for them. Only today, we must translate the importance of a union for farm workers into the language of the 1980s. Instead of talking

---

disposable: available

page 7

Used with permission from Odell Education

170 about the right to organize, we must talk about protection against sexual harassment in the fields. We must speak about the right to quality food and food that is safe to eat. I can tell you the new language is working, the 17 million are still there. They are responding not to picket lines and leafleting alone, but to the high-tech boycott of today, a boycott that uses computers and direct mail and advertising techniques, which has revolutionized business and politics in recent years. We have achieved more success with a boycott in

175 the first 11 months of 1984 than we achieved in the last 14 years, since 1970.

The other trend that gives us hope is the monumental growth of Hispanic influence **P22** in this country. And what that means is increased population, increased social and economic clout and increased political influence. South of the Sacramento River, Hispanics now make up now more than 25 percent of the population. That figure will top

180 30 percent by the year 2000. There are now 1.1 million Spanish-**surnamed** registered voters in California. In 1975, there were 200 Hispanic elected officials at all levels of government. In 1984, there are over 400 elected judges, city council members, mayors, and legislators. In light of these trends, it's absurd to believe or to suggest that we are going to go back in time as a union or as a people.

185 The growers often try to blame the union for their problems, to lay their sins off on **P23** us, sins for which they only have themselves to blame. The growers only have themselves to blame as they begin to reap the harvest of decades of environmental damage they have brought upon the land: the pesticides, the herbicides, the soil fumigants, the fertilizers, the salt deposits from thoughtless irrigation, the ravages of years

190 of unrestrained poisoning of our soil and water. Thousands of acres of land in California have already been irrevocably damaged by this **wanton** abuse of nature. Thousands more will be lost unless growers understand that dumping more and more poison from the soil won't solve their problems on the short or on the long term.

---

surname: the family or last name   **wanton**: careless, undisciplined

page 8

P24

Health authorities in many San Joaquin Valley towns already warn young children
195 and pregnant mothers not to drink the water, because of nitrates from fertilizers
which has poisoned the ground water. The growers have only themselves to blame for an
increasing demand by consumers for higher-quality food, food that isn't tainted by toxics,
food that doesn't result from plant mutations or chemicals that produce red luscious-
looking tomatoes that taste like alfalfa. The growers are making the same mistake
200 American automakers made in the '60s and '70s when they refused to produce small
economical cars and opened up the door to increased foreign competition.

P25

Growers only have themselves to blame for increasing attacks on the publicly
financed handouts and government welfare: water **subsidies**, mechanization
research, huge subsidies for not growing crops. These special privileges came into being
205 before the Supreme Court's "one person, one vote" decision, at a time when rural
lawmakers dominated the legislature and the Congress. Soon, those handouts could be in
jeopardy as government searches for more revenue and as urban taxpayers take a closer
look at front programs and who they really benefit. The growers only have themselves to
blame for the humiliation they have brought upon succeeding waves of immigrant
210 groups that have sweated and sacrificed for a hundred years to make this industry rich.

P26

For generations, they have **subjugated** entire races of dark-skinned farm workers.
These are the sins of growers, not the farm workers. We didn't poison the land. We
didn't open the door to imported produce. We didn't covet billions of dollars in
government handouts. We didn't abuse and exploit the people who work the land. Today
215 the growers are like a punch-drunk old boxer who doesn't know he's past his prime. The
times are changing; the political and social environment has changed. The chickens are
coming home to roost, and the time to account for past sins is approaching.

---

subsidies: money granted by the
government

subjugate: to control; to make submissive

page 9

Used with permission from Odell Education

Updated June 2013

ODELL EDUCATION

I am told these days farm workers should be discouraged and pessimistic. The Republicans control the governor's office and the White House. There is a

220 conservative trend in the nation. Yet, we are filled with hope and encouragement. We have looked into the future and the future is ours. History and inevitability are on our side. The farm workers and their children and the Hispanics and their children are the future in California, and corporate growers are the past. Those politicians who ally themselves with the corporate growers and against farm workers and the Hispanics are in for a big

225 surprise. They want to make their careers in politics; they want to hold power 20 and 30 years from now. But 20 and 30 years from now, in Modesto, in Salinas, in Fresno, in Bakersfield, in the Imperial Valley and in many of the great cities of California, those communities will be dominated by farm workers and not by growers, by the children and grandchildren of farm workers and not by the children and grandchildren of growers.

P27

230 These trends are part of the forces of history which cannot be stopped. No person and no organization can resist them for very long; they are inevitable. Once social change begins it cannot be reversed. You cannot un-educate the person who has learned to read. You cannot humiliate the person who feels pride. You cannot oppress the people who are not afraid anymore. Our opponents must understand that it's not just the union

235 we have built -- unions like other institutions can come and go -- but we're more than institutions. For nearly 20 years, our union has been on the cutting edge of a people's cause, and you cannot do away with an entire people and you cannot stamp out a people's cause. Regardless of what the future holds for the union, regardless of what the future holds for farm workers, our accomplishments cannot be undone. *La causa*, our

240 cause, doesn't have to be experienced twice. The consciousness and pride that were raised by our union are alive and thriving inside millions of young Hispanics who will never work on a farm.

P28

page 10

Like the other immigrant groups, the day will come when we win the economic and political rewards, which are in keeping with our numbers in society. The day will

245 come when the politicians will do the right thing for our people out of political necessity and not out of charity or idealism. That day may not come this year. That day may not come during this decade, but it will come someday. And when that day comes, we shall see the fulfillment of that passage from the Book of Matthew in the New Testament: "The last shall be first, and the first shall be last." And on that day, our nation shall fulfill its

250 creed, and that fulfillment shall enrich us all. Thank you very much.

P29

page 11

Used with permission from Odell Education

Common Core ELA Curriculum

EXPEDITIONARY LEARNING

GRADE 7, MODULE 2A: UNIT 2, LESSON 2

Commonwealth Club Address Structure Anchor Chart

Central claim: Our union will forever exist as an empowering force among Chicanos in the Southwest. That means our power and our influence will grow and not diminish. (P15)

Paragraphs	1–7	8–15	16–21	22 and 27	23–26	28 and 29
Main claim	Farmworkers have faced difficult living and working conditions. Chávez's own experience showed him that, and he decided to organize the union to empower farmworkers in general and Chicanos in particular.			The other trend is that Latinos have more influence politically because they are empowered and their numbers are growing.		
Connection to central claim What is the purpose of this section? How does this one section contribute or add to the text as a whole?				Our power and influence will grow because we vote.		

GRADE 7, MODULE 2A: UNIT 2, LESSON 2

··

Text-Dependent Questions for Paragraphs 1–7

Name:		Date:	

Questions	Write the answer to each question in the left-hand margin of the text. Be brief; you do not need to use complete sentences.
1. After reading P2: What story and images does Chávez tell to begin his speech?	
2. After reading P3: What does Chávez say about the working conditions of the farmworkers?	
3. After reading P5: How does Chávez know about the living conditions of the farmworkers?	
4. After reading P6 and P7: What does Chávez want to do about the conditions of farmworkers?	

EXPEDITIONARY
LEARNING

GRADE 7, MODULE 2A: UNIT 2, LESSON 2

Forming Evidence-Based Claims Graphic Organizer for Paragraphs 1–7

Name: _____

Date: _____

CLAIM

Chávez asserts that farmworkers face difficult and unfair living and working conditions, and that he decided to organize the union to empower the workers in particular and the Chicano people in general.

POINT 1

Chávez asserts that farmworkers face difficult and unfair living conditions and working conditions.

EVIDENCE

EVIDENCE

POINT 2

Chávez decided to organize the union to empower the workers in particular and the Chicano people in general.

EVIDENCE

EVIDENCE

Adapted from Odell Education.

GRADE 7, MODULE 2A: UNIT 2, LESSON 3

Entry Task

Name:		Date:	

Please look at the images and then answer the questions below.

1. What do you notice/wonder about these pictures?

_____

_____

_____

2. How do these pictures connect with the Chávez speech you began reading yesterday?

_____

_____

_____

Common Core ELA Curriculum

GRADE 7, MODULE 2A: UNIT 2, LESSON 3

Rhetoric Toolbox Anchor Chart

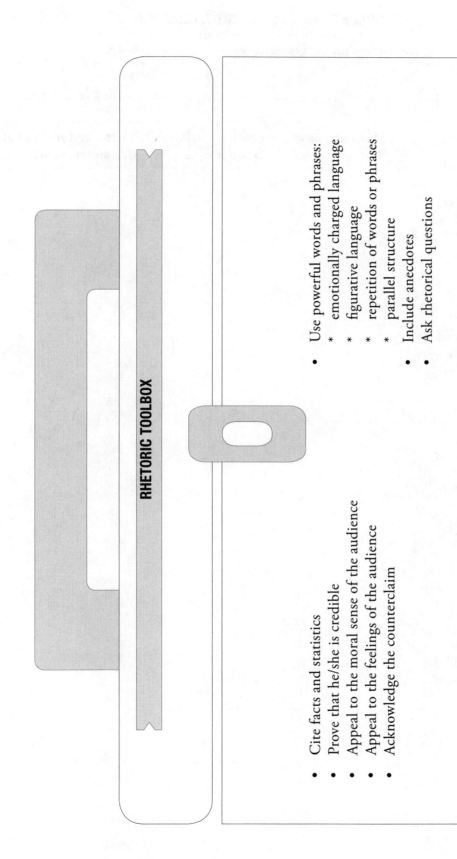

RHETORIC TOOLBOX

- Cite facts and statistics
- Prove that he/she is credible
- Appeal to the moral sense of the audience
- Appeal to the feelings of the audience
- Acknowledge the counterclaim

- Use powerful words and phrases:
    * emotionally charged language
    * figurative language
    * repetition of words or phrases
    * parallel structure
- Include anecdotes
- Ask rhetorical questions

GRADE 7, MODULE 2A: UNIT 2, LESSON 3

Text-Dependent Questions for Paragraphs 8–15

Name:		Date:	

Questions	Write the answer to each question in the left-hand margin of the text. Be brief; you do not need to use complete sentences.
1. After reading P11 and 12: How did the UFW affect other Hispanics from all walks of life?	
2. After reading P13: What is the counterclaim here? What do you expect him to say to dispute this counterclaim in P14?	
3. After reading P14: This paragraph explains the accomplishments of the UFW. List three accomplishments, considering both tangible (things you can see and hear) and intangible (how people feel) accomplishments. Mark the rhetorical question. In the right margins, write down how this question helps him develop his claim.	
4. After reading P15: What will be the future of the UFW?	

Common Core ELA Curriculum

EXPEDITIONARY
LEARNING

GRADE 7, MODULE 2A: UNIT 2, LESSON 4

Forming Evidence-Based Claims Graphic Organizer for Paragraphs 8–15

Name:

Date:

CLAIM

What is a claim that Chávez makes about the UFW in Paragraphs 8–15?

EVIDENCE

EVIDENCE

EVIDENCE

EVIDENCE

Adapted from Odell Education

GRADE 7, MODULE 2A: UNIT 2, LESSON 6

···

Text-Dependent Questions for Paragraphs 16–21

Name:		Date:	

Use Paragraphs 16–21 of Chávez's Commonwealth Club Address to answer these questions.

Questions	Write the answer to each question in the left-hand margin of the text. Be brief; you do not need to use complete sentences.
1. Why did the UFW stop the boycott in 1975?	
2. What word does Chávez repeat in Paragraph 17? How does that help him develop the claim in this paragraph?	
3. In Paragraphs 18 and 19, Chávez criticizes Governor Deukmejian. For what does he criticize him?	
4. In Paragraph 20, what are the "tragic events" Chávez refers to? Why do these events make a boycott necessary?	
5. In Paragraphs 20 and 21, what evidence does Chávez offer to support his claim that the boycott will be successful?	

Common Core ELA Curriculum

EXPEDITIONARY
LEARNING

Updated June 2013

GRADE 7, MODULE 2A: UNIT 2, LESSON 6
....
Homework: Text-Dependent Questions for Paragraphs 23–26

Name:		Date:	

Use Paragraphs 23–26 of Chávez's Commonwealth Club Address to answer these questions. Notice that you should write your answers on this paper, not on the speech.

Questions	Answer
1. After reading P23: Chávez says that the growers are now "reaping the harvest" of decades of actions. To "reap the harvest" means to gather a crop you have grown. What "crop" did the growers plant?	
2. After reading P24: What evidence does Chávez offer of the harm caused by the growers' use of toxic chemicals?	
3. After reading P26: What language does Chávez use in this paragraph to describe the growers? How does this language help him develop his claim about the growers?	
4. After reading P23–26: What is the main claim of this section?	
5. What connections do you see between the claim of Paragraphs 23–26 and the central claim of the speech?	

Name:		Date:	

Directions: Here is one of your learning targets for this unit: "I can analyze the structure of Chávez's speech and explain how each section contributes to his central claim." In the next lesson, you will demonstrate how well you have reached this target on the End of Unit Assessment. You will read a new speech by Chávez and analyze its structure.

What has helped you progress toward meeting this standard?

_____

_____

_____

_____

What questions do you still have?

_____

_____

_____

_____

What will you do to be successful on this assessment?

_____

_____

_____

_____

Common Core ELA Curriculum